# DISCOVER AND DO!

# HUMAN BODY

Written by Jane Lacey

Published in 2023 by Enslow Publishing, LLC
29 East 21st Street, New York, NY 10010

Copyright © 2021 Franklin Watts, a division of Hachette Children's Group

**Editor:** Katie Dicker
**Series Designer:** Rocket Design (East Anglia) Ltd

All rights reserved. No part of this book may be reproduced
in any form without permission in writing from the publisher, except by a reviewer.

Manufactured in the United States of America

CPSIA compliance information: Batch #CSENS23: For further information contact
Enslow Publishing LLC, New York, New York at 1-800-398-2504.

Please visit our website, www.enslowpublishing.com. For a free color catalog of all our high-quality books,
call toll free 1-800-398-2504 or fax 1-877-980-4454.

Cataloging-in-Publication Data

Names: Lacey, Jane.

Title: Human body / Jane Lacey.

Description: New York : Enslow Publishing, 2023. | Series: Discover and do! | Includes glossary and index.

Identifiers: ISBN 9781978530621 (pbk.) | ISBN 9781978530645 (library bound) | ISBN 9781978530638 (6pack) | ISBN 9781978530652 (ebook)

Subjects: LCSH: Human body--Juvenile literature. | Human anatomy--Juvenile literature. | Human physiology--Juvenile literature.

Classification: LCC QP37.L334 2023 | DDC 612--dc23

Picture credits:

t=top b=bottom m=middle l=left r=right

Shutterstock: NoPainNoGain cover/title page l, Sedova Elena cover/title page r, matrioshka 4 and 18b, Artisticco 5tl, 8t and 28t, Lorelyn Medina 5tr, 18t and 31m, Leria Kaleria 5b, 22b and 31b, Riccardo Mayer 7l, Biscotto Design 8, studiolaut 9t, olga boat 9bm, Victor Brave 9br, sciencepics 10b, Puwadol Jaturawutthichai 10bm and 30b, Alena Che 11t, zhu difeng 11b, Anton Albert 11b, stockfour 11b, Distinctive Images 11b, Minerva Studio 11b, StockSmartStart 13t, Robsonphoto 14t, MDGRPHCS 14b, ranicle 16t, GoodStudio 16, AizenStudio 20t, Explode 20b, estherpoon 22t, l i g h t p o e t 24t, Sudowoodo 24b and 31t, Aleksangel 24b, Monkey Business Images 26t, N.Savranska 26b, Rene Jansa 27bl, Petrenko Andriy 27bm, Zdravinjo 27br, Utekhina Anna 27mr; Getty: Yayasya 6, ikryannikovgmailcom 7r, 29tr and 30t, FatCamera 12t and 32, jack0m 12b and 29br, Image Source 27m.

All design elements from Shutterstock.
Craft models from a previous series by Q2AMedia.

# DISCOVER AND DO!

# HUMAN BODY

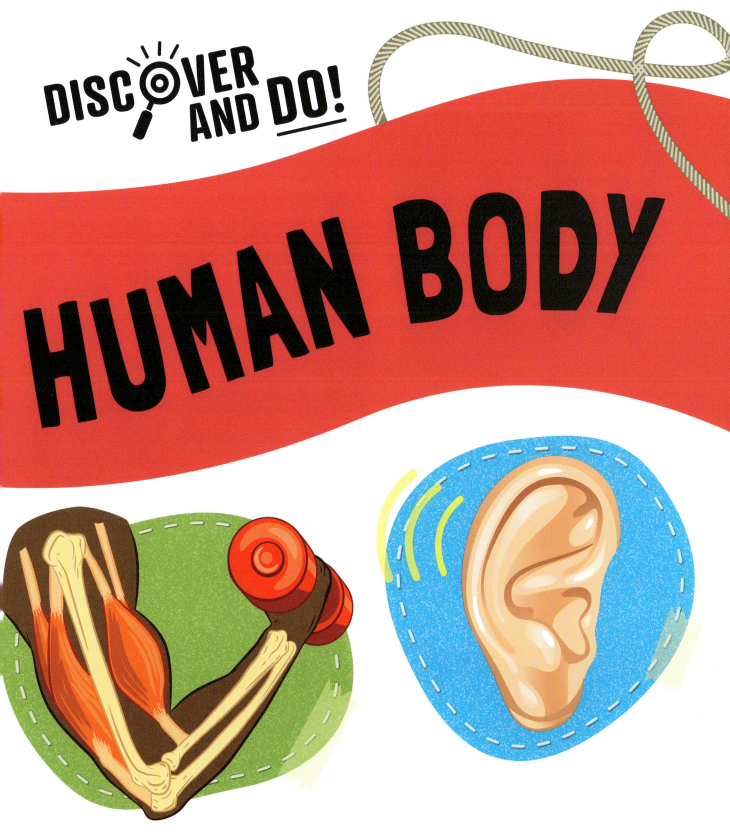

Written by Jane Lacey

# Contents

YOUR BODY . . . . . . . . . . . . . . . . . . . . . . . . . . . 6

A HEALTHY BODY . . . . . . . . . . . . . . . . . . . . . 8

BRAIN AND NERVES . . . . . . . . . . . . . . . . . . 10

HEART AND CIRCULATION . . . . . . . . . . . . 12

BREATHING . . . . . . . . . . . . . . . . . . . . . . . . . 14

SKELETON AND BONES . . . . . . . . . . . . . . . 16

MUSCLES AND MOVEMENT . . . . . . . . . . . . 18

DIGESTION . . . . . . . . . . . . . . . . . . . . . . . . . 20

SKIN . . . . . . . . . . . . . . . . . . . . . . . . . . . . . . 22

SENSES . . . . . . . . . . . . . . . . . . . . . . . . . . . . 24

LIFE CYCLE . . . . . . . . . . . . . . . . . . . . . . . . . 26

GLOSSARY . . . . . . . . . . . . . . . . . . . . . . . . . 28

QUIZ AND FURTHER INFORMATION . . . . . 30

INDEX . . . . . . . . . . . . . . . . . . . . . . . . . . . . . 32

Words that appear in **bold** can be found in the glossary on pages 28–29.

# YOUR BODY

You are a type of animal called a human. Humans have a body with parts that work together so you can grow, learn, eat and drink, **breathe,** and move around.

## Different and the same

Everyone is unique, which means no two people are exactly the same. Your shape and size, the color of your skin, eyes, and hair and the sound of your voice are some of the things that help people to recognize you. We are all unique, but our bodies work in the same way, and we all need the same things to stay healthy, to learn, and to grow.

This group of people shows that humans all vary. They have different body shapes and different colored hair and skin.

# A healthy body

Your body needs water, food, exercise, and rest to be healthy. You can help to keep your body healthy by drinking plenty of water, choosing food that is good for you, staying active, and making sure that you get enough sleep.

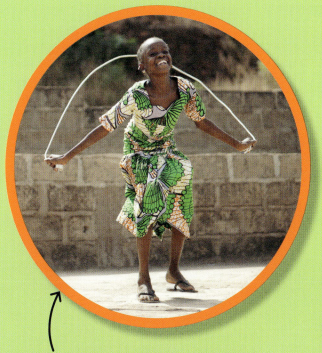

When you exercise, you help your body to be healthy and strong.

# Under the skin

Under your skin is a **skeleton** made up of bones. Your bones protect the soft **organs** inside you. Each organ has a particular job to do. Your lungs, for example, are organs that help you to breathe and your stomach is an organ that helps you to **digest** food. With the help of your brain, your organs work together to keep you alive and well.

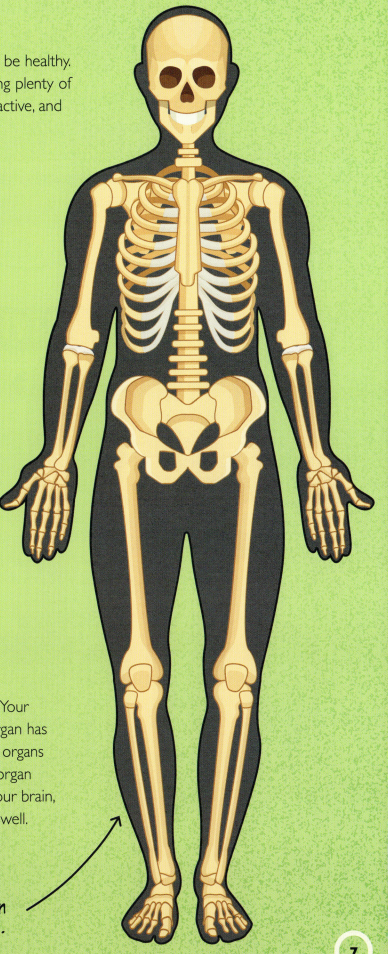

This is what your skeleton looks like under your skin.

# A HEALTHY BODY

If you have a healthy body, you feel well. A healthy body is always growing and repairing itself. It fights **germs** and heals itself if it is hurt. To do this, it uses a lot of **energy**.

*This plate shows some of the different foods you can eat to stay healthy.*

## Healthy eating

Food is the fuel your body burns to give you energy. Fruit and vegetables keep your skin and bones healthy. Bread, pasta, and cereals give you energy. Meat, fish, cheese, beans, and nuts help your body to grow and repair itself. You need some healthy fats and a little salt every day. Your body also needs plenty of water.

## Exercise and rest

Exercise, such as swimming, biking, and running, helps to keep your body healthy. It makes your heart and lungs work hard and keeps your bones and muscles strong. Your body works hard all day, so rest is important, too.

*There are lots of different types of exercise you can do to stay healthy.*

## ACTIVITY

# DESIGN A "LET'S STAY HEALTHY!" PAMPHLET

What would you put in a pamphlet giving children and adults ideas on how to stay healthy?

**2 Exercise**

Walk or bike to school at least once a week.

Learn a new skill such as swimming, biking, or skipping.

Take your dog for a walk (if you have one) or ask a friend or family member to walk with you.

**3 Rest**

Curl up with a good book.

Go to bed on time to get enough sleep.

Here are some examples you could include:

**1 Food**

Choose water instead of sugary drinks when you are thirsty.

Try a new healthy food once a week.

Eat at least five servings of fruit and vegetables every day.

Make sure you get plenty of sleep to be ready for the new day ahead.

# BRAIN AND NERVES

Your brain is the part of the body you learn with and it controls everything you do. Instructions are carried between your brain and the other parts of your body along pathways called **nerves**.

## Brain power

Your brain is soft. It is protected by your skull, the strong bone that gives your head its shape. Each part of your brain has a job to do. You use your brain to think. Your brain also controls how your body works.

## Sending messages

Nerves run from your brain along your spinal cord and spread out around your body. Messages travel along your nerves to tell your brain what your body is doing. Your brain sends messages back to tell your body how to react.

The brain is the body's control center. It has three main parts.

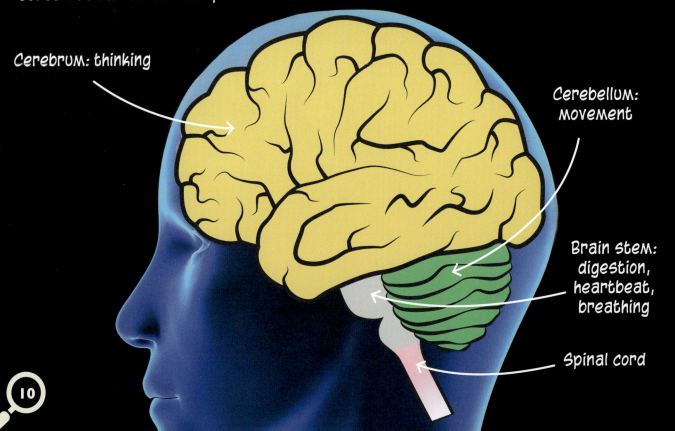

Cerebrum: thinking

Cerebellum: movement

Brain stem: digestion, heartbeat, breathing

Spinal cord

## Learning new skills

You learn new skills when your brain remembers something new. When you learn to ride a bike, for example, practice helps your brain to learn how to do it. Messages pass from your body to your brain and back again, until the new skill becomes easier.

Riding a bike is a skill that you need to practice.

# ACTIVITY

## TEST YOUR MEMORY

**You will need:**
- card stock
- scissors
- **10 pictures of faces cut from magazines**
- glue
- pen
- timer

**1** Cut out 10 playing card-sized rectangles and 10 strips of card stock the same width. Glue a face on each card.

**2** Make up a name for every face and write it on the back of the card and again on a strip of card stock.

**3** Lay out five cards, face upwards. Put their name card under each one.

**4** Ask a friend to study the cards for one minute. Then lay the five cards and names down again in a different order. Can your friend match the faces to the names? Check the name on the back of each card.

Mrs. McDuff   Otis   Peter   Maya   Mr. Brown

**5** Shuffle the cards and lay out six or more. Is it easier when your friend has seen the cards before?

# HEART AND CIRCULATION

The heart and **blood vessels** are the organs that carry blood all around your body. This movement is called **circulation**. Your blood delivers oxygen and the good stuff from your food, called **nutrients**, and collects **waste**.

When you exercise, your heart rate increases to pump more oxygen-filled blood to your muscles to keep them going!

## Beating heart

Your heart is a powerful muscle. It squeezes itself to push blood around your body. Your heart has two pumps. The left pump sends blood full of **oxygen** through blood vessels called **arteries** to your whole body.

When it has delivered the oxygen and nutrients, the blood travels back through blood vessels called **veins** into the right pump. From here it is pumped into the lungs to collect oxygen again.

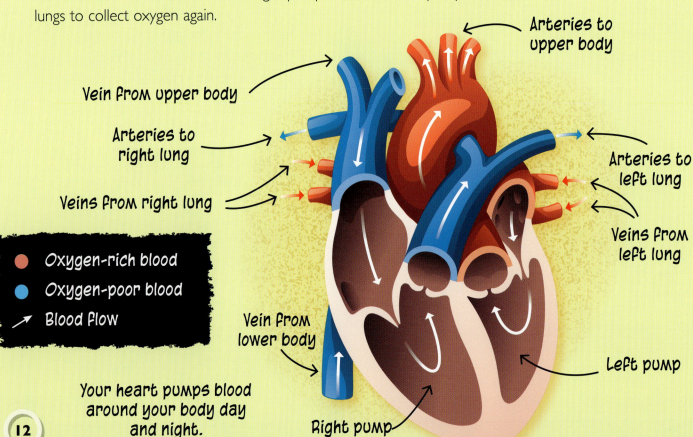

Your heart pumps blood around your body day and night.

## Feeling your pulse

Every time your heart pumps blood into your arteries, they bulge a little. You can feel this "pulse" in the arteries in your wrist and neck. When you exercise, your heart beats faster. It beats more slowly when you are resting.

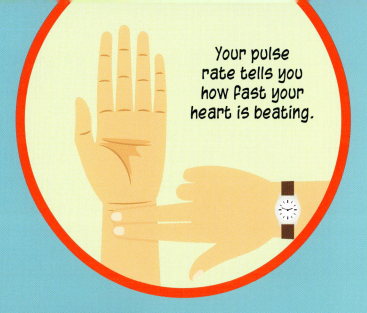

Your pulse rate tells you how fast your heart is beating.

# ACTIVITY

## TAKE AND "SEE" YOUR PULSE

**You will need:**
- **sticky tack**
- **drinking straw**
- **timer**

**1** Find the pulse in your wrist by feeling for it with the fingers of your other hand.

**2** Push a blob of sticky tack gently onto the spot where the pulse feels strongest, so it stays in place. Now push one end of the straw into the sticky tack so it stands upright.

**3** Lie your arm flat on a table and watch the straw twitch with each pulse beat. How many times does the straw twitch in one minute?

Take your pulse at different times of day. For example, when you have just woken up, after running upstairs or after a meal. What differences do you notice?

13

# BREATHING

Oxygen is a gas in the air that your body needs to stay alive. Your nose, **airways**, lungs, and breathing muscles are the body parts you use to breathe in oxygen and take it into your body.

When you breathe out on a cold day, you see your warm breath in the air.

## In and out

You breathe in (inhale) air through your nose and mouth. It goes down your **windpipe** and into your lungs where the oxygen passes into your blood. A waste gas called **carbon dioxide** passes from your blood to your lungs. You breathe out (exhale) this gas.

## Breathing muscles

Your breathing muscles work automatically to pull and push air in and out of your lungs. When you breathe in, muscles widen your chest and lungs to suck air in. When you breathe out, your chest and lungs get smaller and push air out again.

Your windpipe branches off into the left and right bronchus and then smaller passageways called bronchioles.

Windpipe

Right bronchus

Left bronchus

Bronchioles

# ACTIVITY

## MAKE A MODEL LUNG

Ask an adult to help you with this activity.

You will need:
- **2-liter plastic bottle**
- **balloon**
- **plastic bag**
- **scissors**
- **rubber band**
- **strong tape**

**1** Ask an adult to cut the top third off the plastic bottle and remove the cap.

**2** Pull the open end of the balloon over the bottle spout. Push the balloon down inside the bottle.

**3** Cut a circle of plastic from the plastic bag, bigger than the cut end of the bottle. Cover the open end of the bottle with the plastic and hold it with a rubber band. Now tape it firmly in place with strong tape.

**4** With your thumb, push the plastic up gently to make less space around the balloon. Watch the balloon shrink as air goes out of it. Now release the pressure to make more space around the balloon and watch air move back into it.

The balloon is like your lungs — they fill when the space around them expands (gets bigger) and empty when the space around them contracts (gets smaller).

# SKELETON AND BONES

Your skeleton is a strong frame. A fully grown human has 206 bones. Your skeleton holds you upright, gives you your shape, and allows you to move. It protects soft organs such as your brain, heart, and lungs.

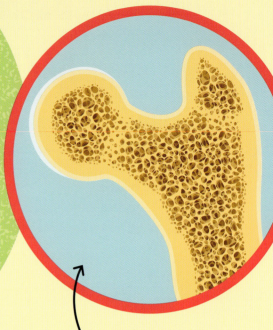

Bones contain living tissue that regularly renews itself as you grow.

## Joints

The bones in your skeleton are joined together in places called joints. Many joints move. Your elbows, knees, and fingers have **hinge joints**. They bend and straighten like the hinge of a door. Your hip and shoulder joints swivel in every direction.

## Bones

A baby's bones are soft and flexible. As you grow, your bones become harder. Bones are light and strong. The outside layer is smooth and hard. The middle layer looks like a sponge. If you break a bone, over time it can mend itself.

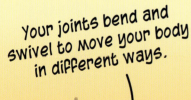

Your joints bend and swivel to move your body in different ways.

# ACTIVITY

## MAKE A MODEL BONE AND TEST ITS STRENGTH

**You will need:**
- **colored paper**
- **scissors**
- **tape**
- **paperback books**

**1** Cut two pieces of paper into thirds lengthways to get six strips of paper about 8 inches x 4 inches (20 cm x 10 cm). Roll one strip into a short tube, and close it with tape.

**3** Cut the remaining paper strips lengthways to make smaller strips about 1.5 inches x 4 inches (4 cm x 10 cm). Roll each one into a long tube and close with tape.

**4** Pack the inside of the large tube with the smaller tubes standing upright. Test the tube for strength again. How many books can it support before it collapses this time?

**2** Stand the tube upright on a flat surface. Place a book across the top of it. How many books will the tube hold before it collapses? Remake the tube if needed.

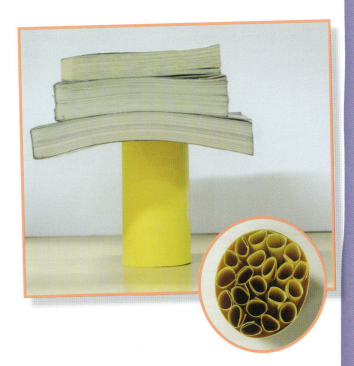

The new tube is much stronger. Like a bone, it is also light. It has a hard outside and closely-packed tubes inside. The tubes strengthen the bone, but keep it light.

# MUSCLES AND MOVEMENT

Your body is moved by muscles. Muscles move your bones by pulling them. You use muscles in your face to smile, frown, and blink. Your heart is a muscle that pumps blood around your body.

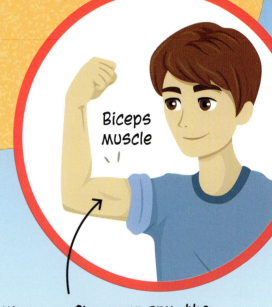

When you flex your arm, the biceps muscle in the top of your arm tenses and shortens.

## Moving around
Strong cords called tendons attach muscles to your bones. Some muscles are attached to two bones, stretched across a joint. When you bend your knees, for example, different muscles move your legs and **flex** your knee joints.

## Strong muscles
Muscles that you use a lot can become bigger and stronger. Those you don't use much can become smaller and weaker. Skiers and cyclists have strong muscles in their legs. You can keep your muscles strong and healthy by getting plenty of exercise.

Strong muscles in the legs of cyclists help them to pedal faster.

# ACTIVITY

## PLAY "BEND AND BALANCE"

A game for two players to test your muscle strength and balance.

**You will need:**
- sheet of white card stock
- 4 sheets of colored paper (red, yellow, blue and green)
- 4 sheets of colored card stock (red, yellow, blue and green)
- scissors
- pen

**1** Cut out four playing card-sized pieces of white card stock and four playing card-sized pieces of red, yellow, blue, and green. card stock. Cut a large circle from each piece of the colored paper.

**2** On the white cards write:
- right foot • left foot
- right hand • left hand

Shuffle the white cards and put them face down in a pile. Shuffle the colored cards and put them in a pile next to the white cards.

**3** Player 1 stands on some grass, or a soft mat, with the four colored circles around them. Player 2 picks up a white card (ex. right hand), then picks up a colored card (ex. green). Player 1 puts their right hand on the green circle.

**4** Player 2 calls out all the white cards, with a color, and player 1 follows the instructions. Keep calling the cards until player 1 loses their balance and falls over! Then it's Player 2's turn.

The winner is the player who can make the most moves without losing their balance.

19

# DIGESTION

When you eat, your body breaks down your food into tiny pieces. This process is called digestion. Nutrients from your food are sent all around your body in your blood. Nutrients give your body energy to work, grow and repair itself.

You should brush your teeth after breakfast and last thing at night.

## Teeth and chewing

Your food's journey starts in your mouth. First, you chew your food into small pieces. You need strong, healthy teeth for chewing. You should brush your teeth carefully and visit your dentist regularly.

Esophagus

Stomach

Small intestine

Large intestine

## The journey

When you swallow your food, muscles squeeze it through your esophagus into your stomach. Your food is mashed into a runny soup. It moves to the small intestine where most nutrients pass to your blood. In the large intestine, water is absorbed to produce waste called **feces**.

# ACTIVITY

## MAKE A DIGESTION DIARY

Find out how long it takes for you to feel hungry again after you have eaten.

**You will need:**
- notebook
- pencil
- ruler
- pens or colored pencils

**1** Make a grid on the first page of your notebook, like the one shown below, and fill it in. Make a similar page for two or three days of the week.

**2** Write a story of the journey of one of your meals.

### Amazing journeys starring... my breakfast!

I ate breakfast too quickly and didn't chew my food well so I got hiccups. They lasted a half an hour! Lumpy food went down my esophagus and into my stomach where...

## MONDAY

|  | Time | Food | Comment |
|---|---|---|---|
| **BREAKFAST** | 7:00 | cereal, banana, orange juice  | Ate too quickly – hiccups! |
| hungry | 10:15 |  |  |
| snack | 10:30 | bran muffin, milk  | Yum! |
| hungry | 12:30 |  | Football practice. Starving! |
| **LUNCH** | 12:45 | chicken pot pie, green beans, yogurt, water  | Nice and filling. |
| hungry |  |  |  |
| snack |  |  |  |
| hungry |  |  |  |
| **DINNER** |  |  |  |

21

# SKIN

Your skin is your body's biggest organ. Like all the organs in your body, it has particular jobs to do. It covers and protects your whole body and gives you your **sense** of touch.

## Amazing skin

Your skin renews and repairs itself all the time. An outer layer of dead skin falls off when your skin rubs against your clothes or when you wash. Look at your fingertips through a magnifying glass and you will see fine lines called fingerprints. No two people in the world have the same fingerprints.

## In the sun

Our skin color is caused by a natural color (or pigment) called melanin. It helps to protect us from the sun's rays. Our skin makes more melanin in sunlight and turns darker. But too much sunlight can burn and damage our skin. Always wear sunscreen on hot days to protect your skin from the sun's rays.

*Fingerprint scans are used to identify a particular person.*

*People have different shades of skin. Darker shades have more melanin, which protects the skin from the sun.*

# ACTIVITY

## TAKE FINGERPRINTS

You will need:
- pencils
- pencil sharpener with a place for shavings
- 3 sheets of white card stock
- ruler
- black pen
- double-sided tape
- scissors
- magnifying glass

**1** Collect pencil shavings in the sharpener. Tip the shavings onto a sheet of card stock. Collect the pencil dust.

**2** On each remaining sheet of card stock, draw two rows of five boxes. Label the top row "left hand" and the bottom row "right hand." Write your name on one card, and your friend's name on the other.

**3** Stick a small piece of double-sided tape to each square. Keep the protective paper on the top side.

**4** Press the fingertip of your little finger into the black pencil dust. Pull off the protective paper from the first square and press your blackened fingertip onto the sticky tape. Take a print of all your fingers in the same way.

**5** Stick your friend's fingerprints to the other card. Examine them with a magnifying glass.

Secretly make a fingerprint on another piece of sticky tape. Can your friend match it to the correct fingerprint on your card?

# SENSES

Your body has five senses: sight, hearing, smell, touch, and taste. They tell you what is going on around you. You sense things with different parts of your body.

Without our senses it would be difficult to cross a road safely.

## Sense organs

We see with our eyes, hear with our ears, smell with our noses, touch and feel with our skin, and taste with our tongues. Information detected by these **sense organs** is turned into signals that are sent to the brain to tell us what is happening.

## Staying safe

Our senses help us stay safe. We use our eyes and ears to see and hear traffic so we can cross the road safely. We feel heat coming from a fire so we know not to touch it. A bad smell tells us to keep away from harmful germs. A nasty taste tells us when our food has gone bad.

When you eat toast, you use all five senses to know it is good to eat.

You taste it.

You hear it crunch.

You see the shape and color.

You smell a delicious smell.

You feel it is warm.

# ACTIVITY

## MAKE A SENSORY SOCK PUPPET

Make a toy to entertain a young child using sight, sound, movement, and touch.

*Ask an adult to help you with this activity.*

You will need:
- **brightly colored sock**
- **pieces of brightly colored felt**
- **scissors**
- **needle and thread**
- **scraps of material and yarn**
- **small paper bag**

**3** Sew on scraps of material with interesting textures and yarn for hair.

**1** Turn the sock so the sole is facing upwards. Push your hand inside so the heel is on top of your hand. Push the toe of the sock back between your fingers and thumb to make a mouth.

**2** Cut ears, eyes and a nose from the pieces of felt. Ask an adult to help you sew them onto the sock. You can copy the shapes shown here or make up your own.

**4** Put your hand inside the paper bag and pull the sock over the top. Make a mouth as before. When you move the mouth it will make a crunchy sound!

Entertain a child you know with your sensory puppet! Let them touch it to feel the different textures.

25

# LIFE CYCLE

Human babies are born and they grow up into children. Children become adults and they may begin new **life cycles** by having children of their own. Over time, adult humans grow older and eventually die.

This father is helping his one-year-old child to learn to walk.

## Growing up

A human baby starts life inside its mother's **womb**. After about nine months, it is ready to be born. A baby needs to be looked after all the time. It grows into a toddler and learns to walk and talk. Children go to school and learn to do many more things.

## Getting older

As adults get older, they start to change in several ways. Hair color fades and skin becomes lined. Muscles and bones become weaker. Older people have a lot to offer. They have learned a great deal during their lives.

Older people can teach children and young people a lot of new things.

## ACTIVITY

# MAKE A PERSONAL ALBUM

Keep a record of growing up.

**You will need:**
- album or scrapbook
- photographs of yourself
- scissors
- tape
- glue
- pens
- ruler
- colored paper
- height chart

**1** Collect photographs of yourself growing up. Stick them in the album in order and label them with your age and when they were taken. Find out facts about yourself and write them in. For example, how much you weighed at birth and when your first tooth came in.

**2** On a new page, stick a photograph of yourself now. Write in your height, weight, how many teeth you have, and your favorite things such as your favorite color, book, music, sport, etc.

**3** Add a new page every few months or on every birthday.

**4** Record your growth on a height chart and see how much you grow each year. Look back through your album.

How much have you changed over the years?

# Glossary

### airways
Airways are the tubes that connect your nose and throat to your lungs. The air you breathe in and out travels through your airways.

### arteries
Arteries are blood vessels that take blood from the heart to different parts of the body.

### blood vessels
Blood vessels are tubes that carry blood through your heart and all around your body.

### breathe
To breathe is to take air into your lungs and to let it out again. We need to breathe to stay alive.

### carbon dioxide
Carbon dioxide is a gas in the air. Your body does not need carbon dioxide so you get rid of it when you breathe out.

### circulation
Circulation is the movement of blood through the body, through blood vessels and the heart.

### digest
When your body digests food, it breaks it down, uses the nutrients from it, and gets rid of waste.

### energy
Energy is the power to do work. Food, water, and oxygen give your body the energy it needs to grow and work.

### feces
Feces is the solid waste from your food that your body gets rid of when you go to the bathroom.

### flex
When you flex your limbs or joints, you bend them.

### germs
Tiny germs in the air or in food can cause diseases that make you ill if they get into your body.

### hinge joint
A hinge joint lets bones open and shut in one direction, like the hinge of a door.

### life cycle
A life cycle describes the way life goes around and around like a circle. Humans are born, they grow, they make new life like themselves so life can go on, and they die.

### nerves
Nerves are pathways that carry messages between your brain and your body.

## nutrients
Nutrients are the parts of your food that your body uses to grow, stay healthy, and repair itself.

## organ
An organ is a part of your body that has a particular job to do. For example, your lungs are the organs that you use to breathe.

## oxygen
Oxygen is a gas in the air. Your body takes in oxygen when you breathe air into your lungs.

## sense
A sense is one of the five ways you pick up information from the world around you. Your five senses are seeing, hearing, tasting, touching, and smelling.

## sense organs
Your sense organs are the parts of your body you use to sense the world around you – your eyes, ears, tongue, skin, and nose.

## skeleton
A skeleton is a frame made up of bones. It gives humans their shape and protects parts of their body.

## veins
Veins are blood vessels that take blood to the heart from different parts of the body.

## waste
Waste is what is left over and not wanted. For example, a waste gas is what we breathe out when oxygen has been taken out of the air we breathe into our lungs.

## windpipe
Your windpipe is a tube between your throat and your lungs. Air travels through your windpipe when you breathe.

## womb
A womb is the part of a woman's body where a baby grows before it is ready to be born.

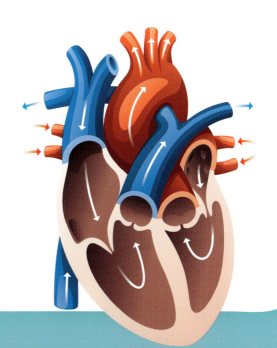

# Quiz

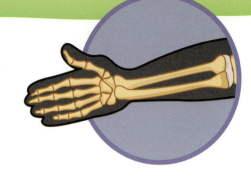

**1** Which of the below does your body need?

a) water
b) food
c) exercise
d) rest

**2** In what order do you breathe in air?

a) windpipe
b) nose/mouth
c) bronchioles
d) bronchus

**3** Which two are correct?

a) arteries carry blood away from your heart
b) arteries carry blood to your heart
c) veins carry blood away from your heart
d) veins carry blood to your heart

**4** Your brain has:

a) one main part
b) two main parts
c) three main parts
d) four main parts

**5** How many bones does an adult have?

a) 106
b) 206
c) 116
d) 216

**6** What is your body's biggest organ?

a) skin
b) heart
c) lungs
d) brain

**7** In what order do you digest food?

a) esophagus
b) small intestine
c) stomach
d) large intestine

**8** How long does a baby stay in the womb?

a) eight months
b) nine months
c) three months
d) a year

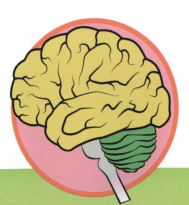

**9** How many senses do you have?

a) two
b) three
c) four
d) five

**10** Which of these are arm muscles?

a) bisons
b) bisects
c) biceps
d) bichettes

ANSWERS 1 all of these! 2 b/a/d/c, 3 a/d, 4c, 5b, 6a, 7 a/c/b/d, 8b, 9d, 10c

# FURTHER INFORMATION

## BOOKS

*A Question of Science: Why don't your eyeballs falls out?* by Anna Claybourne, Wayland

*Boom Science: Human Body* by Georgia Amson-Bradshaw, Franklin Watts

*The Bright and Bold Human Body* by Izzi Howell, Wayland

*100% Get the Whole Picture: Human Body* by Paul Mason, Wayland

## WEBSITES

All about the human body: www.bbc.co.uk/bitesize/topics/zcyycdm

Amazing body facts:
www.natgeokids.com/uk/discover/science/general-science/15-facts-about-the-human-body

Take a closer look inside!: www.tenalpscommunicate.com/clients/siemens/humanbodyOnline

Find out more and test yourself: www.dkfindout.com/uk/human-body

# Index

blood 12, 13, 14, 18, 20
blood vessels 12
bones 7, 8, 10, 16, 17, 18, 26
brain 7, 10, 11, 16, 24
breathing 6, 7, 10, 14

carbon dioxide 14

digestion 7, 10, 20, 21

ears 24
energy 8, 19, 20
eyes 6, 24

food 6, 7, 8, 9, 12, 20, 21, 24

germs 8, 24

heart 8, 10, 12, 13, 16, 18

intestines 20

joints 16, 18

life cycle 26
lungs 7, 8, 12, 14, 15, 16

mouth 14, 20, 24
movement 6, 10, 12, 13, 16, 18, 25
muscles 8, 12, 14, 18, 20, 26

nerves 10
nose 14, 24

organs 7, 12, 14, 16, 22, 24
oxygen 12, 14

pulse 13

rest 7, 8, 9, 13

senses 22, 24
skeleton 7, 16
skin 6, 7, 8, 22, 24, 26
stomach 7, 20, 21

teeth 20, 27

waste 12, 14, 20
water 7, 8, 9, 20, 21